I0867286

ENERGY

This book belongs to

____

____

____

____

Wonder House

ENERGY

ENERGY IS WHAT HELPS US TO
SURVIVE

IT HELPS US TO DO WORK AND
KEEPS US ALIVE

ARTIFICIAL LIGHT FROM THE
BULB

OR NATURAL LIGHT FROM THE
SUN

ENERGY MAKES OUR DAYS
BRIGHT AND FUN

POTENTIAL ENERGY ON THE
TOP OF HILL

KINETIC ENERGY IN A MOVING
WINDMILL

USING MECHANICAL ENERGY
WE HAMMER A NAIL

THERMAL ENERGY HELPS US
DRY OUR HAIR

LIGHT, SOLAR, ELECTRICAL,
CHEMICAL AND SOUND

FORMS OF ENERGY ARE
EVERYWHERE TO BE FOUND.

LOOK AT THE KIDS RUNNING AROUND THE PLAYGROUND TIRELESSLY!
THEY DON'T SEEM TO SLOW DOWN. THEY HAVE A LOT OF ENERGY!
THIS BATTERY HAS LASTED FOR A REALLY LONG TIME.
YES, IT STORES A LOT OF ENERGY.
YOU SEEM TIRED! WHY DON'T YOU HAVE THIS ENERGY DRINK?
YES, I NEED TO BOOST MY ENERGY!
THE FOOD WEB THAT WE'RE A PART OF, IS A GIANT NETWORK OF ENERGY BEING TRANSFERRED.
Food Web
BUT WHAT IS ENERGY?

WHAT IS ENERGY?

SUN IS THE MAIN SOURCE OF ENERGY ON THE EARTH.

ENERGY IS USUALLY DEFINED AS THE CAPACITY OR ABILITY TO DO WORK.
HERE, WORK MEANS MOVING AN OBJECT, OR CHANGING IT IN SOME WAY WHEN A FORCE IS APPLIED TO IT.

PLANTS GET ENERGY FROM THE SUN. THIS HELPS THEM GROW BIG AND STRONG.

HUMANS GET ENERGY BY EATING FRUITS, MEATS AND VEGETABLES

ANIMALS GET ENERGY BY EATING PLANTS, FRUITS OR OTHER ANIMALS.

WHEN WE EAT FOOD, WE GAIN THE ENERGY TO DO WORK.

SOURCES OF ENERGY

THE ENERGY WE USE TO POWER THINGS AROUND US COMES FROM DIFFERENT SOURCES. THESE SOURCES CAN BE DIVIDED INTO TWO KINDS—RENEWABLE AND NON-RENEWABLE.

RENEWABLE SOURCES OF ENERGY

A NATURAL SOURCE OF ENERGY THAT CAN RESTORE ITSELF QUICKLY IS CALLED RENEWABLE SOURCE. RENEWABLE SOURCES OF ENERGY ARE:

- ABUNDANT
- CONSTANTLY REPLENISHED
- SUSTAINABLE
- ENVIRONMENT FRIENDLY

EXAMPLES OF RENEWABLE SOURCES OF ENERGY

SOLAR ENERGY
ENERGY THAT COMES FROM THE SUN

WIND ENERGY
ENERGY OF THE WIND THAT CAN BE HARNESSED BY WIND TURBINES

BIOMASS
ORGANIC MATTER SUCH AS CROPS, SEAWEED AND ANIMAL WASTE

HYDROPOWER
ENERGY WE GET FROM THE FORCE OF MOVING WATER

GEOTHERMAL ENERGY
IT COMES FROM THE HEAT GENERATED FROM GEYSERS OR VOLCANOES

NON-RENEWABLE SOURCES OF ENERGY

A NATURAL SOURCE OF ENERGY THAT CANNOT BE REPLENISHED IS CALLED NON-RENEWABLE SOURCE. NON-RENEWABLE SOURCES OF ENERGY:

- ARE LIMITED IN QUANTITY
- ARE NOT SUSTAINABLE
- ARE NOT ENVIRONMENT FRIENDLY
- LEAD TO GLOBAL WARMING

EXAMPLES OF NON-RENEWABLE SOURCES OF ENERGY

HOW DO WE USE ENERGY?

WE USE DIFFERENT KINDS OF ENERGY TO DO DIFFERENT TASKS SUCH AS:

TYPES OF ENERGY

ENERGY CAN BE BROADLY DIVIDED INTO TWO TYPES—POTENTIAL ENERGY AND KINETIC ENERGY.

POTENTIAL ENERGY

THE ENERGY STORED IN AN OBJECT AT REST DUE TO ITS POSITION, ARRANGEMENT OR STATE IS CALLED POTENTIAL ENERGY.

SUCH ENERGY IS NOT YET USED BUT READY TO BE RELEASED.

FOR EXAMPLE

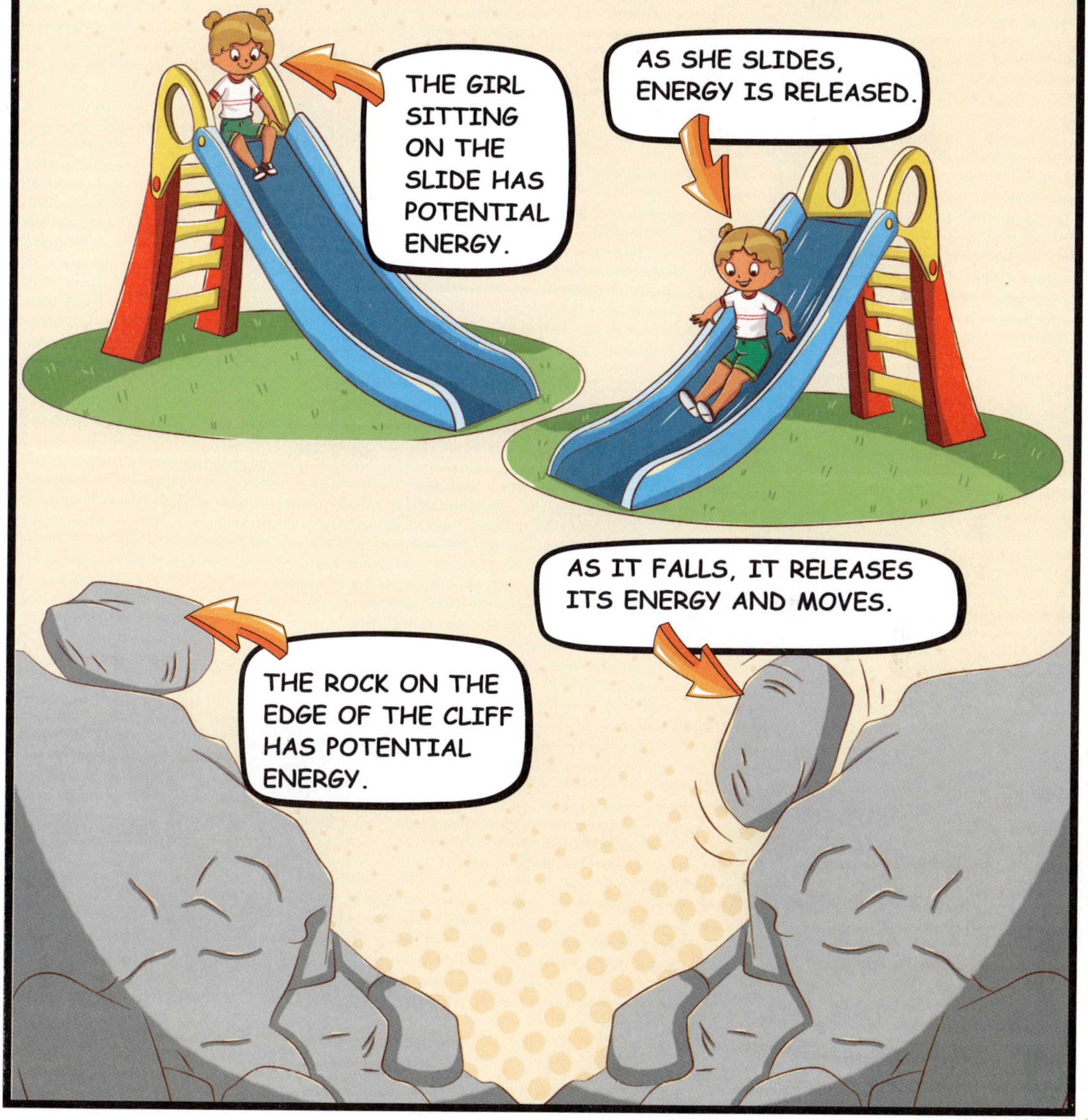

TYPES OF POTENTIAL ENERGY

POTENTIAL ENERGY IS OF MAINLY TWO TYPES—ELASTIC POTENTIAL ENERGY AND GRAVITATIONAL POTENTIAL ENERGY.

ELASTIC POTENTIAL ENERGY

IT IS THE ENERGY STORED IN AN OBJECT WHEN IT IS STRETCHED OR COMPRESSED.

FOR EXAMPLE

SPRING

THE SPRING IS STATIC.

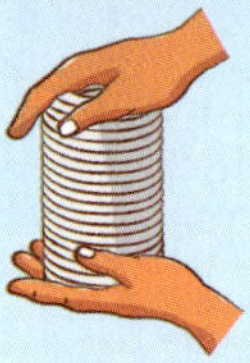

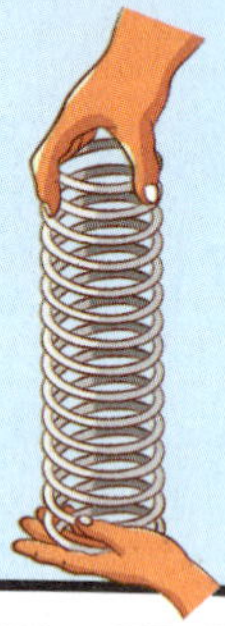

WHEN COMPRESSED OR STRETCHED, IT GAINS ELASTIC POTENTIAL ENERGY

IN A POGO STICK

THE SPRING WHEN PRESSED DOWN BY THE GIRL'S WEIGHT GAINS ELASTIC POTENTIAL ENERGY

WHEN THE SPRING CAN'T BE COMPRESSED ANY MORE, IT WILL COME BACK TO ITS ORIGINAL SHAPE.

THE ENERGY IT RELEASES PUSHES THE POGO STICK—AND THE GIRL—OFF THE GROUND.

LONGBOW
WHEN THE STRING IS STRETCHED IT GAINS ELASTIC POTENTIAL ENERGY
WHEN THE STRING IS RELEASED, IT WILL CAUSE THE ARROW TO SHOOT FORWARD.
SLING SHOT
RUBBER BAND
STRETCHED
RELEASED

GRAVITATIONAL POTENTIAL ENERGY
IT IS THE ENERGY STORED IN AN OBJECT WHEN IT IS POSITIONED AT A HEIGHT.
FOR EXAMPLE
A DIVER ON THE DIVING BOARD
A CYCLIST ON A STEEP HILL
IN BOTH THE CASES, GRAVITY WOULD WORK TO PULL THEM DOWN.
THE HIGHER AND HEAVIER THE OBJECT, THE MORE GRAVITATIONAL POTENTIAL ENERGY IT HAS.
MORE GRAVITATIONAL POTENTIAL ENERGY BECAUSE HE IS AT A GREATER HEIGHT
MORE GRAVITATIONAL POTENTIAL ENERGY BECAUSE HE WEIGHS MORE

KINETIC ENERGY
THE ENERGY OF AN OBJECT DUE TO ITS MOTION IS CALLED KINETIC ENERGY.
MOTION OF PLANETS
A FLYING AIRPLANE
A MOVING CAR
A MOVING PENDULUM
MOVING BLADES OF A WINDMILL
WHEN AN OBJECT IS AT REST, ITS KINETIC ENERGY IS ZERO.

FORMS OF ENERGY

ENERGY EXISTS IN DIFFERENT FORMS.

MECHANICAL ENERGY

ENERGY THAT INVOLVES MOVEMENT IS CALLED MECHANICAL ENERGY.

CHARGE A PHONE
LIGHT A BULB
ELECTRICAL ENERGY
ENERGY GENERATED BY THE MOVEMENT OF ELECTRIC CHARGES (CALLED ELECTRONS) IS CALLED ELECTRICAL ENERGY. ELECTRICAL ENERGY IS USED TO:
RUN ELECTRIC VEHICLES
RUN ELECTRICAL APPLIANCES

LIGHT IS GIVEN OFF BY THINGS SUCH AS:
SUN
LASER
LIGHT BULBS
STARS
IT IS ALSO USED BY PLANTS TO PRODUCE THEIR FOOD BY A PROCESS CALLED PHOTOSYNTHESIS.
GLOW WORMS
LIGHT ENERGY
LIGHT IS A FORM OF ELECTROMAGNETIC RADIATION WHICH WE CAN SEE. IT IS PRODUCED WHEN ATOMS OF AN OBJECT HEAT UP. LIGHT IS THE FASTEST THING IN THE UNIVERSE.
LIGHT IS THE ONLY FORM OF ENERGY VISIBLE TO HUMAN EYE.
LIGHT ENERGY HELPS US TO SEE.

THERMAL ENERGY

THERMAL ENERGY IS GENERATED WHEN SOMETHING IS HEATED OR BURNED. HEATING PRODUCES A RISE IN THE TEMPERATURE OF AN OBJECT.

SOURCES OF HEAT ENERGY

WE USE HEAT ENERGY FOR:

CHEMICAL ENERGY

CHEMICAL ENERGY IS A FORM OF ENERGY STORED IN BONDS OF ATOMS AND MOLECULES.

IT IS RELEASED WHEN THE BONDS BETWEEN MOLECULES BREAK APART AND REARRANGE THEMSELVES DURING A CHEMICAL REACTION.

SOURCES OF CHEMICAL ENERGY

THE FOOD WE EAT ALSO CONTAINS CHEMICAL ENERGY. AS THE BONDS IN ATOMS OF FOOD ITEMS BREAK DURING DIGESTION, ENERGY IS RELEASED. THIS ENERGY KEEPS US WARM, HELPS US TO GROW AND DO DIFFERENT TASKS LIKE:

USES OF CHEMICAL ENERGY
FLASH LIGHT TURNS ON
PETROL BEING FILLED
FOOD GETS COOKED ON GAS
CLOCK RINGING
USING COMPUTER MOUSE
BATTERY OPERATED REMOTE
CARRY LUGGAGE
RUNNING VEHICLES
MAKES THE WATCH WORK

SOUND ENERGY

SOUND IS A FORM OF ENERGY THAT WE CAN HEAR. IT IS CAUSED BY VIBRATION OF PARTICLES IN AN OBJECT.

SOUND MOVES THROUGH AIR OR OTHER MEDIUMS IN THE FORM OF WAVES.

WE EXPERIENCE MANY EXAMPLES OF SOUND ENERGY IN OUR EVERYDAY LIFE. THESE ARE:

ENERGY TRANSFER

ENERGY TRANSFER IS THE MOVEMENT OF ENERGY FROM ONE PLACE OR OBJECT TO ANOTHER.

FOR EXAMPLE

A MAN PUSHING A CART

THE MAN PUSHES THE CART.

ENERGY IS TRANSFERRED FROM THE MAN TO THE CART AND THE CART STARTS MOVING.

KICKING A FOOTBALL

THE BOY KICKS THE FOOTBALL.

ENERGY FROM THE BOY IS TRANSFERRED TO THE FOOTBALL AND IT MOVES.

BOILING WATER

WHEN PLACED ON THE STOVE, HEAT FROM THE STOVE IS TRANSFERRED TO THE WATER THROUGH THE PAN MAKING IT BOIL.

ENERGY TRANSFORMATION

ENERGY TRANSFORMATION HAPPENS WHEN ENERGY IS CONVERTED FROM ONE FORM TO ANOTHER.

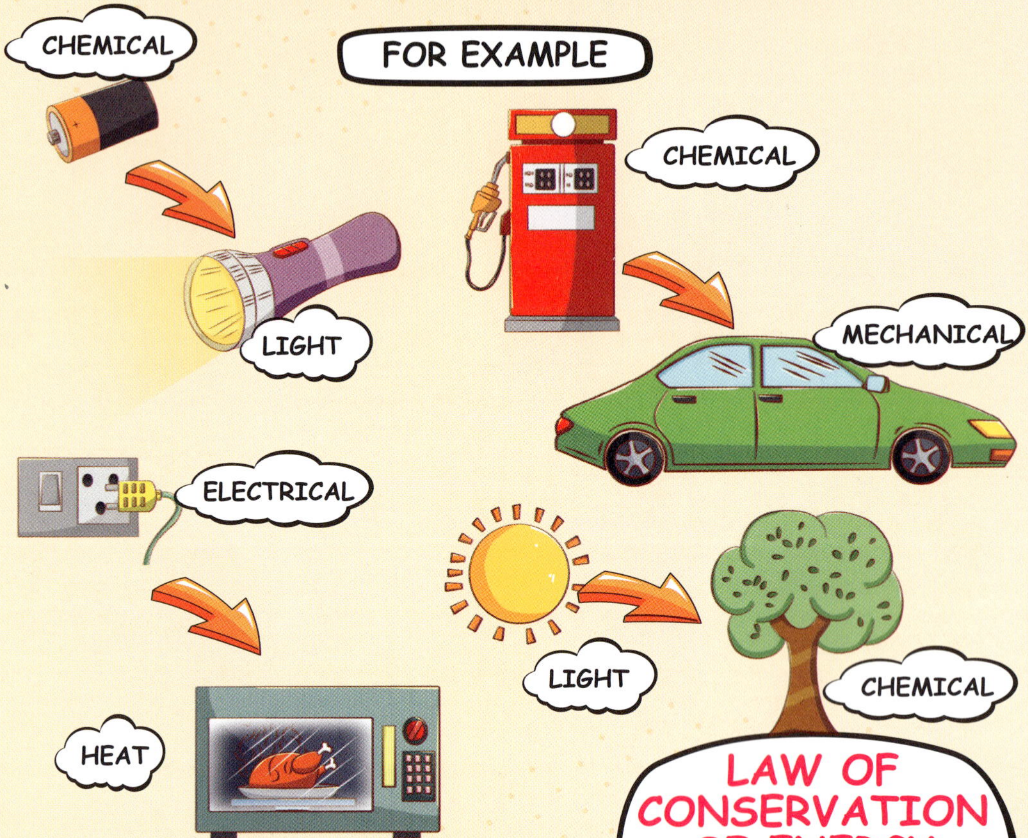

ENERGY TRANSFER AND ENERGY TRANSFORMATION ARE TWO DIFFERENT PROCESSES. IN ENERGY TRANSFER, THE FORM OF ENERGY REMAINS THE SAME WHEREAS WHEN ENERGY IS TRANSFORMED, IT CHANGES ITS FORM.

LAW OF CONSERVATION OF ENERGY

WHILE ENERGY CAN BE TRANSFORMED FROM ONE FORM TO ANOTHER, THE TOTAL AMOUNT OF ENERGY REMAINS THE SAME. THIS IS CALLED THE LAW OF CONSERVATION OF ENERGY.

ENERGY CAN NEITHER BE CREATED NOR DESTROYED.

LET'S BE ENERGY EFFICIENT!

BEING ENERGY EFFICIENT MEANS USING ENERGY WISELY AND ALSO REDUCING OUR OVERALL DEMAND FOR ENERGY.

WAYS TO BE ENERGY EFFICIENT

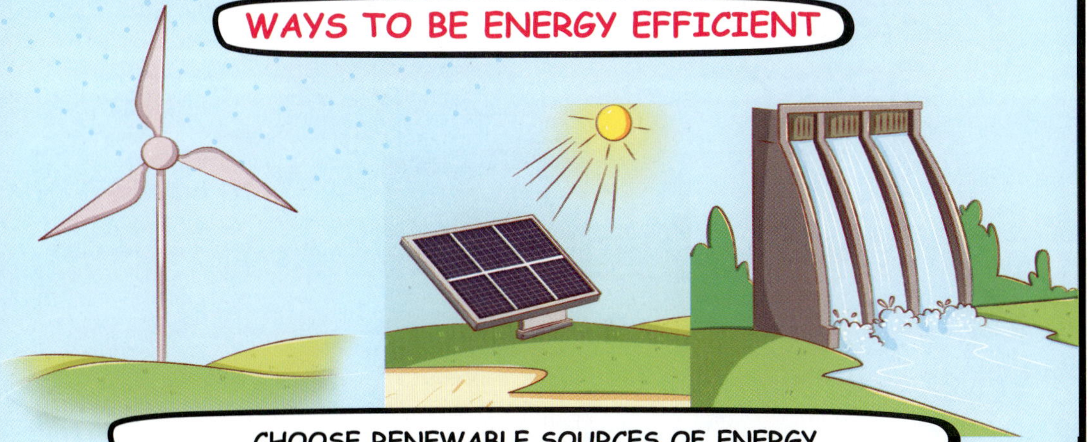

CHOOSE RENEWABLE SOURCES OF ENERGY

SWITCH OFF APPLIANCES AND TURN OFF LIGHTS WHEN NOT IN USE.

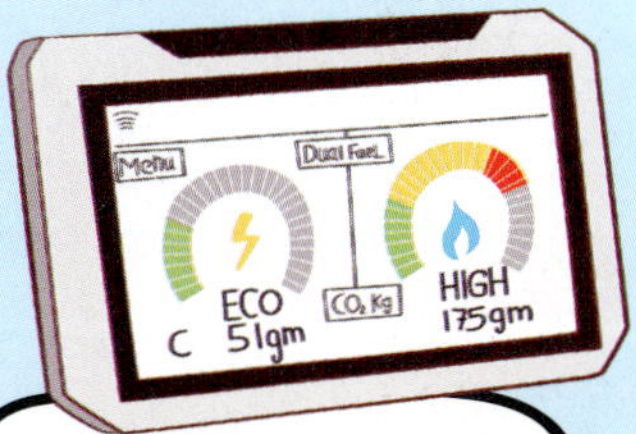

TRACK YOUR ENERGY USAGE FROM TIME TO TIME

USE LED LIGHTS WHICH ARE ENERGY EFFICIENT

SWITCH TO ENERGY EFFICIENT APPLIANCES

65 °F
KEEP THERMOSTAT AT LOW TEMPERATURE
WASH CLOTHES IN COLD WATER
SWITCH TO DOUBLE GLAZING
USE MICROWAVE WHILE COOKING
COOK WITH LID ON
CLEAN/REPLACE AIR FILTERS REGULARLY
USE NATURAL LIGHT
DRESS ACCORDING TO WEATHER